How to Write Good

JOHN VORHAUS

Copyright © 2013 John Vorhaus

All rights reserved.

ISBN: 1482554739
ISBN-13: 978-1482554731

to everyone who has the itch

books
by John
Vorhaus

Non-fiction

The Comic Toolbox: How To Be Funny Even If You're Not
Creativity Rules! A Writer's Workbook
Killer Poker: Strategy and Tactics for Winning Poker Play
Killer Poker Online
The Killer Poker Hold'em Handbook
Poker Night
The Strip Poker Kit
Killer Poker Online/2
Killer Poker No Limit
Killer Poker Shorthanded (with Tony Guerrera)
Decide to Play Great Poker (with Annie Duke)
Decide to Play Drunk Poker
The Little Book of Sitcom

Fiction

Under the Gun
The California Roll
The Albuquerque Turkey
World Series of Murder
Lucy in the Sky
The Texas Twist

1. HOW TO WRITE GOOD

This book will teach you how to write good. That's a fact. You may already believe it because you've embraced the title, the joke of it, but also its hidden meaning. "Anyone who writes a book about writing," I figure you figure, "must know enough about grammar to write 'how to write *well*.' Well, if he knows correct usage and yet chooses not to use it, then it must be with purpose. *Maybe this guy knows something.*"

Well, yes, yes he does. For one thing, he knows how to read minds; he knows that 90 percent of everything everyone thinks is pretty much the same stuff, so the trick of reading other people's minds is really just getting better at reading your own. (Boy, here comes a convoluted sentence – get ready for it.) I figure you figure what I figure you figure because if I were you I would be figuring the exact same thing. (Told ya. Convoluted as hell.) Mind reading is especially useful for driving characters through story, but we'll get to that later.

Back to the title, back to how to write good.

Mostly what I want the title to convey is *whimsy*. As I grow as a writer, I think more and more that whimsy is one of the strongest cards I can play. I'm not talking about funny writing, but rather a writer's playfulness – her willingness to make choices. Like my choice just here to make *she* the default pronoun for this book. Choice is made. I don't second guess. I move on. As a writing strategy, it's a pretty darn useful one, so let's put it on a line by itself.

Choice is made. Don't second guess. Move on.

I had an idea to write a book called *How to Write Good.* I thought that the title might be sexy and alluring to a certain type of writer, one already predisposed to appreciate whimsy. You, having self-selected as that sort of writer (you're still here, aren't you?) might now be interested in seeing how to use whimsy as a tool for getting your writing moving better.

But let's be careful about the word "better." Let's be sure we know what we mean by that. To me, in this context, *better* is largely just *faster*. I consider myself a "better" writer when my process is more efficient, when I'm getting more writing done. I *don't* consider myself a "better" writer when I'm sitting there staring at the blank page. That's when I consider myself a worse writer, or worse, no writer. That's always the point I want to get past. And whimsy is a tool I can use there. Why? Because whimsy suspends value judgments. Whimsy says that any choice is a good choice. Whimsy explores ideas just for fun. Whimsy doesn't care about broken bits of writing or storytelling. Or grammar. Or syntax. Or complete sentences. Whimsy plans to fix everything later. Whimsy, out of sheer whimsy, thinks of as many ways as it can to express whimsy. Whimsy knows there's more than one path through story. Whimsy says *what the fruck*. (And whimsy makes *fruck* a word.) Whimsy knows the secret of how to write good.

Here it is.

Write *bad*.

Fail on the page. And fail on the page. And fail on the page. Let whimsy help you. Let whimsy validate any choice you make, because any choice you make keeps you moving forward on the page. You know (because whimsy tells you) that you'll definitely be going back to fix things later, but that's not your job right now. Right now your job is exactly this simple:

Keep writing.

Keep failing. Then fail some more. And some more after that. Then guess what? Soon you'll start failing less. Why? Because you'll be improving your *process*. Driven by whimsy, your choices will start coming easier and faster. Now you're saving all the time you used to waste second-guessing yourself, and investing that time in writing instead. You're pushing that text out onto the page and of course with each new sentence you write, writing sentences is something you're gonna get better at doing. (And see what a hash I made of that sentence? That's it — that's the whimsy. That's me not caring if I make a fool of myself on the page. Go to school on that. It's so great to be a writer who doesn't fear to be a fool. And I have dined out on that particular morsel for years.)

I think I know where you're at now. You're not as productive as you want to be. Not as prolific. Not as at ease with your craft. Not yet its master, for sure. In the back of your mind you hear a panicked little voice that clamors,

I'm falling behind in my existence!

How do I know you hear that voice? Because I hear it all the frucking time! I've heard it all my life. I experience it as exactly this: **the gap between the writer I am and the writer I want to be.** I'm furiously interested in closing that gap. You are, too, I know; that's why you're here. And here's the thing I want to tell you. You *will* close the gap. I have. Not all the way. But some. And consistently more and more over time.

And I can show you how.

When I started my so-called "writing" so-called "career," I couldn't write for fifteen minutes at a time without falling apart. Fear retarded my growth, impeded my progress, stopped me cold. Day in and day out, I had this weird practice of not-writing, of doing everything I could think of except putting words on the page. I was simply too afraid to put words on the page, too afraid to commit to my choices, any choices at all. I was always afraid that I'd make the wrong ones. I hadn't yet learned this stunning truth:

In writing, there are no wrong choices.

Muse upon that for a second. Decide for yourself if you think it's true. If you happen not to think so, I would here ask you to pretend otherwise. Imagine that it's true and see what impact that new point of view has on how you approach your work. I suspect that its impact will be exactly this: You will become more free 'n' frisky on the page, simply as a function of your reduced or eliminated fear of being wrong.

And that's what we call a **useful fiction**. A useful fiction is a lie we tell ourselves to serve some strategic purpose (like getting to be more free 'n' frisky on the page). We know it's a lie, but pretend it's not, for the sake of some strategic gain.

I have some experience in this area. Often, a young writer on a writing staff I'm running will come to me and ask, "Do you believe in me? Do you think I can do this job?" I always answer yes, and I always identify my answer as a useful fiction, i.e., I tell her I might be lying. The truth is, I don't know if she can do the job or not – probably, that's what we're there to find out – but I do know that if I don't express my faith, real or imagined, I will in no way be serving her efforts to become the writer I need her to be. So I explain about the useful fiction and propose that we both believe she can do the job unless and until evidence demonstrates otherwise. That's a useful fiction disguised as a self-fulfilling prophecy, and it's a very handy tool to have. You can use it on yourself. Just fake it till you make it.

(If you recognize *fake it till you make it* as a buzz-phrase from Alcoholics Anonymous or other types of addiction recovery programs, that's not by accident. All real writers are addicted to writing. Get used to it. It's not the end of the world.)

(For the record, we're not trying to shed our addiction, we're just trying to manage it better.)

These days I can't wait to write. I feel no fear at all. I allow every idea I can think of to have (or at least contend for) a life on the page. I make a choice and move on. Make another choice and move on. Make another choice and move on. I know that every choice I make is a choice I can unmake later – *but not if I don't keep moving on! !* Because the first goal of every writing project, for this completist writer at any rate, is to **get the first draft done***,* and that won't happen in the presence of fear. So I kill fear with whimsy, like killing snails with salt, and the words keep flowing out. Now, this doesn't mean that I don't judge. Right this very minute, the editorial me wonders if "killing snails with salt" isn't too graphic an image for what I'm driving at here. The editorial me wants to cut it. But whimsy says, "Ya know what? Let's leave it for now. We can always fix it later." And then the words keep flowing out.

See how that works?

Try how that works.

I don't mean that rhetorically. I mean it like this: Right here and right now, sit down and try how that works. That's an important part of this book – the most important part, in fact. These are *tools,* Jules, and they don't work if we don't use 'em. So when I say write, I mean *write*, right? It'll do you no harm, I swear.

I'm aware that this freedom to choose and not care puts me on a certain slippery slope. Liberated from the need to judge, I might become completely indiscriminate. I might let every word I write live in this book exactly as I blooted it out of my brain onto the page. You'll never know. Did I edit that sentence? (Did I edit *that* one?) It sure looks like I didn't. It looks like I'm letting any idea and every idea live on the page, with no thought to economy, no thought to style, no thought to quality, no thought to how these words will later be judged. I'm just writing. I'm working on my active practice.

My **active practice of writing.**

Do you have that? An active practice of writing? If you don't, it's a goal of this book to help you build one. It's another goal of this book to use the word *completist* completely gratuitously and almost completely incorrectly. *Mission already accomplished!* But that other mission, the one of guiding you to an active practice of writing, that's going to take me more than 20,000 words. I'm psyched for that, though. I hope you are, too.

Want to hear something funny? This paragraph you're reading now, I started it a whole different way. I wrote three or four sentences I didn't like and then went back and deleted them. I broke my own rule about not judging! This tells me two things about me. First, that the gap will never completely close. There will always be definable space between the writer I am and the one I want to be. I will always wish for a better, cleaner, more completely unself-conscious practice of writing than I have. I will always want more whimsy, more pure freedom of choice. But also, I'm getting better at my craft. I'm getting better at knowing what a bad sentence looks like, and at knowing when, let's face it, I'm just going down a wrong road.

Whimsy lets you try things out. Judgment lets you make stuff go away.

But again, we have to be careful. If we spend too much time checking out the sentence we just wrote, we're too slow in getting to the sentence we'll next write. And right now the next sentence is much more important than the last.

What we can strive for is this: Edit, but don't edit. That sounds important and Zen, I know, but how, exactly, does it work?

Like this. Judge a sentence by this test only: Does it get you to the next one? If yes, keep writing. If no, fix what needs to be fixed and move on. But the thing is, again, *move on.* Get that first draft finished. Major revisions – real fixes – will come later, and that's part of your active practice, too. But right here and right now, I want you to appreciate the true freedom I have granted myself in these first few pages. By establishing my default setting as *whimsy,* I've given full license to everything and anything I can think of. I have given free rein to my voice. Which brings me to one of the most important things I think I know about being a writer, so important that its worth recording in both bold *and* italics:

Keep giving them you until you is what they want.

You make the rules. You get to decide how you sound. You get to write good. You get to decide what good writing is. The more comfortable you become with making those arbitrary choices – the ones that make you cringe and think, *Jeez, they'll never buy this!* – the sooner those arbitrary choices become your voice. I sell whimsy hard because to me whimsy comes easy. It's useful to ask yourself what comes easy to you. Are you funny? Yay you. Do you have a good ear for dialogue? A knack for description? A natural gravitational pull toward cliffhangers? Where lie your strengths? Take inventory of these, for these are the cornerstones of your voice.

Take that inventory now, if you please. And don't imagine you don't have strengths. Everyone has tons.

I know a young writer who's quite gifted in story. I don't know what it is, he just gets it. He knows how events play out. His dialogue ear is terrible now, so that while the events of his stories are quite authentic and organic, the things his characters say ring phony as a Bolex watch. It's not his fault; it's just where he's at right now. So when you inventory what you're good at, don't for a second lament the things you're bad at. That's just where you're at right now.

Meanwhile, I did it again, I broke my own rule. I was here thinking about how to help you make faster choices to propel your writing forward and I let myself get distracted by a completely irrelevant technical issue: Should I make *keep giving them you until you is what they want* a chapter all by itself? I started fussing with chapter headings and section breaks, and I know this book will need those, but certainly the time for that is not now. I've only just started the thing. How can I *organize* what has yet to be *written?* But the urge is strong. The urge to *fiddle* and not to write. I recognize the urge. I nod to it. I honor it and move on. I undo the formatting mess I've just made and write about what I'm thinking about now.

It's such a freedom to be able to write about what I'm thinking about now. Folks, what you're thinking about now, that's your voice. Be aware of that. Watch yourself work. It's a very important part of your active practice.

See yourself writing.

Study what you do well and strive to do more of it. Study what you do less well and strive to do less. For me that's *stop being distracted by stuff that doesn't matter now.* I know that's another one of those gaps I'll never completely close; however, I can get better. I can *see myself writing* and at least recognize when I'm *not* writing. I'll get distracted again, I know. Of course I will. I'll get distracted, leave the page, stop writing, just as I have done countless times before. But next time – if I see myself writing – I'll recognize the state a little bit quicker. I'll close the gap a smidge. And a smidge more. And a smidge more after that. Soon I will have an effective tool for recognizing that I'm prone to being taken off the page. Over time I will go from:

"Holy crap, I left the page again!" to
"Holy crap, I'm leaving the page again!" to
"Holy crap, I see myself wanting to leave the page!" to
"Holy crap, I'm not leaving the page!"

When you're on the page, you're writing. Good writing, bad writing, doesn't matter. Keep writing. Keep doing that. Trust your choices – not that they're good ones, necessarily, but that they're *yours*. I simply can't stress this enough. As a writer you want to make choices that are *easy* and *fun* for you. You don't want to make choices based on how you think your work will be received or what traffic some mythical market will bear. Audience and market are worthy goals to strive for, but don't be driven by them. Down here on the page, where the only things that matter are the next choice you make and the next sentence you write, you don't want to be thinking about *them*, you want to be thinking about *you*. And you want to make the choices that are easy and fun and reflect who you are. Because that's your voice, and guess what? The thing that ultimately attracts your audience and your market is... *ta da!...* your voice. So keep giving them you until you is what they want.

Let's think about where we are right now, because we're kind of inside a *metalogue,* a type of discourse in which the topic at hand and the means of discussing that topic are reticular (*resembling or forming a network* – and no I didn't know it either until I looked it up). Here's me telling you to write through your voice, and how am I communicating that idea? By writing through mine. I'm demoing the product, if you will. But your voice is nothing like mine. (Well, *something* like mine, if you were drawn to this work through the whimsy.) The freedom you give your voice will be a freedom that plays to your strength. Let's just say for the sake of conversation that you're great at imagining worlds – you can create alien space like nobody's business. At some point in your work, you might find yourself judging one of your choices and saying, *No, that's too alien, too far out. I'll never get away with that.* That's the point where you go wrong. If alien thinking is your strength, then *mo' alien, mo' better*, say I.

Maybe your strength lies in *heart*. Many a writer's strength does. They just see emotion like I see whimsy or my young colleague sees story. So they write heart, heart, heart. Marriage this, divorce that, *Oh, my God, she's cheating on him!* But at some point they're bound to come to a choice they don't feel they can make. *My readers will never let me get away with it.* (Remind me to tell you about the choice I just made.) Trust me, your readers *will* let you get away with it. They *want* you to get away with it. They want you to play to your strengths – give them you – because that's what they've come to desire. And if you think they will never come to desire what you have to give, consider this: They surely never will if they don't get the chance. Give them you. Give them you. Give them you.

If you're having trouble remembering this, you might do what some people do: scrawl it on a sticky – *Give Them Me!* – and post it at your workstation or on your bulletin board or wherever, so that you can see it and be reminded of it every day. It's an antidote to doubt.

I'm a big believer in stickies. Stickies rule. I have one right here on my desk that says *buy more stickies.* That's how much they rule.

Meanwhile, I wanted to tell you about that choice I just made. See, I recognized that I'd used the phrase *get away with it* in back-to-back paragraphs, and that sounded repetitive to me. Now normally in my work I make a very harsh value judgment about repetitive phrases: *I don't like 'em, I don't like 'em, I don't.* At a certain point in every book I write I consider it my job to police and eradicate redundancy. Well, I "saw myself writing" just now. I saw myself applying that value judgment and I said, "Hang on a sec, that judgment doesn't apply here. I can be repetitive if I like. Right now it's part of my voice."

The key phrase there is *right now.* Your voice is not just one thing. Over the course of your career you're going to develop all sorts of strengths and you'll seek and find all sorts of ways and places to apply them. For me it's like, sometimes my work will be half whimsy and sometimes it will be all whimsy. (Very occasionally there's no whimsy at all, but that's rare; I can't help it, the damn whimsy keeps creeping in.)

For me, most of the time, I don't tolerate repetition, but for right here and right now it's okay. And that's what we really mean by whimsy:

For right here and right now it's okay.

Want to know where I am right here and right now? In my mind I'm already selling this book. I'm plotting my Amazon attack, even thinking about cover concepts. (For some reason I see pale yellow. How did that pan out?) Isn't that funny? Three thousand words in and I'm already into *how great will this be when it's done!* Oh, believe me I'm there. I'm thinking about you reading these words and being inspired to sit down and write with a freedom and – I'm going to make this up – a *joie de plume* that maybe you've never felt before. I visualize your writing getting you high. (Which happens for notable scientific reasons that we'll discuss later, I promise.) I foresee you closing the gap between the writer you are and the writer you want to be. I see your active practice of writing, and I get very excited by that.

I'm looking over my own shoulder now, and thinking, *Man, JV, these folks are going to think you're mighty up yourself.* Yes, they might, and yes, I'm afraid of that. I'm afraid that if you think I'm up myself you'll stop liking me and stop coming along for this ride. So now I have a problem. I want to describe you to you, which is something I think I can do, but I don't want to come off as an arrogant prick. Can we trust that I'm not? Can we trust that I'm here to serve? I hope so, because with all due false modesty I do think I'm pretty great.

Didn't see that one coming, did you? Neither did I. It feels like a self-indulgence, a fun little trick I just played. But right now I'm all in the middle of *self-indulgence is its own reward,* so if you expect me to come back later and cut this bit out, don't hold your breath. (Wouldn't it be funny if I did? Then you wouldn't be reading this at all.)

Back to false modesty: The thing is I am pretty great. You're pretty great. Every writer is pretty great every time she sits down to write, because she's fulfilling her purpose. She's being the person she's supposed to be, and the person she wants to be. But if she's going to have something to say – and I think she *does* have something to say – she'll only say it boldly if she thinks she's pretty great. Otherwise, she won't think she deserves to say it, or dares to say it, and that would be a shame.

Say it. *Say it!* Whatever dark secret you're afraid to reveal. *Say it!* Whatever cornball idea you can't help but explore. *Say it!* Whatever bizarre affectation you just thought up. *Say it!* Whatever dumb joke. *Say it!* Whatever scary truth. *Say it.* Say it. Say it all. They won't hate you for it. It's what they come to you for. Or what they'll come to you for eventually. But only if you say it now.

Say it now.

And don't be afraid to say it.

You might start by listing ten dark secrets about yourself, stuff you don't want *anyone* to know. I don't know what's on your list, but I'll bet that every single item there will make great grist for a story, just because it's a dark secret, and so heartfelt. And even if you don't make story stuff out of it, well, that's ten dark secrets about yourself that you just copped to. Tell me that doesn't redound to better self-awareness for you. And tell me that you don't feel more comfortable with your dark secrets for having written them down. Do you know that being more self-aware and more comfortable with your dark secrets are two profound goals of your active practice? You do now. So write now.

So here's me saying, *Say it now,* and driving inspiration as hard as I can. But this begs a certain hurdle: You might not know what *it* is. Blorting your dark secrets is one thing, but what's your *message,* right? What's your higher purpose? That's a good question to ask – a great question to ask – but maybe not the one to ask right now. If you set yourself the goal to change the world with your words, you'll be stalled by your own expectation and aspiration. So let's think about what we want to say in a less highfalutin and a somewhat more practical manner.

What I want to say in this book is *set yourself free to write more.* That's pretty simple. That's an idea I can grasp. It's also one I can own. I certainly don't fear people coming around with pitchforks and torches just because I tried to set some writers free. So I'm on safe ground with my *say it now.* You don't have to be on safe ground, but I must admit it helps.

So what do you want to say now? Doesn't have to be an earth-shaker, just a simple human truth that you think might be helpful to others.

Say it. Write it down. Now you're a writer, yay you.

It's a change of state, you know, from not-writer to writer. It's a line in your life. Which side are you on right now? Are you a writer or a want-to-be writer? Either one is fine. If you're already a writer then you're that much ahead of the game. If you're not yet a writer (as you self-define) then you have something thrilling to look forward to: your transformation. Jeez, who couldn't get psyched about that?

I know exactly when in my life I crossed the line from not-writer to writer. I was twenty years old, lying in bed on the night before I left for Europe on that summer-after-college backpacking thing we all did. As I lay awake, unable to sleep, I had an idea for a song, a "talking blues" like Bob Dylan used to do. And I made a mental note to write it down in the morning. But I knew I wouldn't. I knew I'd be too busy, what with all the leaving for Europe and all. So then I thought, *Better get up and write it down right now.* And that's what I did. And when I was done, I thought, *Son of a gun, I wrote me a song. I didn't know I could do that.* I was so excited; I was high. Naturally I wanted to get high like that again, so I started doing it more. I wrote songs all that summer, all over Europe, and ended up with a chronicle of the trip that I'd certainly not have otherwise had. And then I went on to learn guitar and become a singer-songwriter of a sort, which was my first real "writing" career and which lasted until I learned that there were two things I couldn't do very well: sing, and play guitar. Amazingly, I still know that first talking blues by heart. Want to hear it? Thanks, I thought you'd never ask.

TALKING FOREIGN LANGUAGE BLUES

When I touched down in Luxembourg
I couldn't speak a foreign word.
That talkin' by the residents,
well it didn't seem to make no sense.
S'il vous plait. Chevrolet. Can't understand a word they say.

Pretty girl comes up to me,
points to herself and says, "Marie."
She didn't say another word
but I figured I might go with her.
She squeezed my hand you see. I understand.

We're walking down the avenue,
she looks up, says, "*Parlez vous?*"
I say, "Pardon me, my little doll,

but I don't understand at all."
She just smiled. I shoulda known.

She guides me down the street a spell,
leads me up a long stairwell,
Opens up an apartment door,
says, "Entre-vous, mon-see-yore."
Got curtains on the wall. American flags, ya see.

Well I'm confused, I scratch my head
but then she's lying on the bed.
She looks up and says, "Oui screw?"
Knows some English. Now what do I do?
Real cute. Laying there in her birthday suit.

Well, I figured I might have a go,
that cultural exchange, ya know.
So I strip down and there I stand,
a-showin' her my Marshall Plan.
And it's a ten-point plan.

It was nice I must admit,
and I dozed off for just a bit.
When I woke up though, things turned bad.
She'd run off with all I had.
Europe on 10 Bucks a Day and my
ticket back to the USA.

Yes it's true I did get burned.
Ah, but she give me something in return.
A little gift from sweet Marie,

she left me with the clap, ya see.
Spirochetes. Crippler of young adults.

Don't think I'll go back out there,
across the sea to places where
I can't understand a word they said.
No I'll take Omaha instead.
Sure it's boring. Ah, but it ain't catching.

Oh, man, feel what I'm feeling now! That's something I wrote damn decades ago! That's the *first thing* I wrote! I barely showed it to anyone back then. How do you think I feel about showing it now? Nervous. Very apprehensive. What if you think I suck? Well, I guess I'm safe in that because the me you think sucks is ancient history now. Still, I can tell you that back then that guy *obsessed* over "What if they think I suck?" A lot of writers obsess over that. (My informal poll indicates that all writers do.) God, what if they think you suck?

Well what if they do?

Well, what *will* they do?

I mean, in practical terms, what's the worst that can happen? They won't read what you write. So what? Someone else will. Someone, somewhere will read you and think you don't suck, I promise. And if the worst that can happen is people don't read you, well, hey, aren't they doing that now?

Throw it out the window. See if it lands. That's the basic algebra of writing. Throw it out the window. See if it lands.

Plus you don't know. You never know. You're going to write millions of words in your career. You can't predict which ones will have value, or how they'll even be used. Something I wrote in 1977 just found a new life in 2013. Folks, that's not nothing. That's time travel in a sense, I cryogenically froze a thought in my youth and thawed it out just now. Even if it's only an artifact, and even if it's not "good," it's still interesting. It's an artifact of my past to be inspected and examined. Can someone please tell me how I'd have that artifact available for inspection now if I had never created it back then?

I realize that I'm making an assumption about you. I'm assuming you're a young writer, just starting out, or at least close enough to starting out that helpful books on writing still catch your eye. If you're more experienced than that and you feel I'm telling you things you already know, I apologize. But if you are a young writer – you who are reading these words right now – I'm not surprised. After all, you're who I'm writing for – you're who I want to set free from fear. And if you're reading these words, then that just means I'm doing my job of hitting the target I'm aiming for. It's a job I've gotten better at as I've gone along. And that's the point I'll keep stressing and stressing: *You'll get better as you go along* – if you do just one simple thing.

Keep writing.

Write every day. Every chance you get. Don't worry about outcome. If you're young, you can't *imagine* outcome. Do you think *any* version of my young could have envisioned what I'd be doing with my words in middle age? No way in hell. I didn't believe I'd live this long. I even bet against it. Back then I couldn't see the future. I could barely see the present. And as I've already told you, I could hardly write a word, or anyway that's how it seemed at the time. But I tried, and I kept trying. Oh, trust me, most of what I wrote back then was junk – similar in some sense, I'd guess, to the junk you're writing now. But junk is cool. Junk's a start. And every writer makes a start.

You are on the path, my young friend (or not so young friend). It's the same path we're all on, we writers: the writer's path. Each of us is at our own place on it, and each of us is advancing at our own pace on it. But we all share the same goal: to have an active practice of writing, one that will serve our every dream and ambition to reach out and touch other minds with our minds.

Where you are, I was. Where I am, you will be.

So write it all down. Say what you have to say. Find your voice and then leverage the crap out of it. Don't worry about outcomes. Trust that life is long. Plan to reuse much of what you write in later days and other ways. You will. You'll do that a lot. You'll draw on your own previous resources, return to your recurring themes, take the lessons of past failures and apply them to future success. And all you have to do is keep writing.

Anything.

Freely.

With whimsy.

It's amazing what happens from there.

2. THE WONDERFUL WORLD OF PIVOTS

Okay, let's get down to work.

What I want to talk about now is the ***pivot***, a highly handy tool for developing, tracking and understanding what happens from one story moment to the next. For the sake of this discussion, we'll define it thus:

*A pivot is **a new piece of information that triggers a change in a character's emotional state.***

Pivots are completely scalable. That is, they define story moments as large as *an asteroid is heading for the earth!* and as small as *a teenager discovers a zit.* In the former example, everyone's emotional state changes from *la, la, la, nice day* to *oh, God, we're all going to die!* In the latter case, the teen's emotional state changes from blissful ignorance (of his zit) to despair. Pivots are the fundamental building blocks of most scenes, but *scene* is a bit of a dangerous word, in that it can lead you think about pivots only in the context of TV or film stories, and/or only in the context of scripts. I want you to think of pivots – see them and use them – in every type of story you write, or might want to write, from short to epic, from library to stage to screen. I also want you to think of them in every phase of story development, from conception through final execution. As you'll soon see, this is going to make your writing life a lot easier. So for the sake of this discussion (and isn't this discussion already demanding quite a lot of us?) let's think of pivots as the driving force of scenes, where a *scene* is defined as any story moment you're exploring, big or small, in prose, script or whatever.

So here's a scene, and here's a pivot: *A character is waiting in line at the bank and the bank is held up.* Prepivot, the character feels fine. Postpivot, she feels floor. Can I get away with prepivot and postpivot as words? My whimsy says *why not?* And my status as a promiscuous purveyor of new words very nearly demands it. It looks funny, though: *prepivot*, like it's just begging to be mispronounced. So I feel self-conscious about it. Like I feel self-conscious about the bank robbery example. *Such a dumb example.* I tell myself it doesn't matter, it's just an example. And I let it live for now. There's just no reason to change it now, and every reason to *just… keep… writing.* And I wouldn't even be mentioning it except to point out that our *ideas* and our *feelings* about our ideas come into existence together. No sooner do we have a notion than we have a reaction to it. Managing your feelings about your ideas is a big part of being the writer you want to be, and it comes down to the difference between *thinking* about an idea and *feeling* about an idea, which we may express more simply as:

Evaluate, don't judge.

In evaluating the bank robbery example, for example (an example of an example and now my head is starting to explode), I ask how well it solves the problem it sets out to solve. In this case, it sets out to illustrate a point, and it certainly does that. But *judging* it, now, judging it is more like, *That's stupid. You can do better than that.* When that voice, the judgment voice, has control of my head, no writing gets done. Or you know what? Maybe not. Maybe I accept that as a challenge. *Come on, JV, you can do better.* Hmm. I always thought *evaluation* was good and *judgment* was bad. Now, suddenly, I'm not so sure. It used to be that when I got caught up in judgment I'd get all down on myself and then stop writing. I just realized – I mean *just* realized – that I don't get down on myself anymore. Not to say that it's always Sunnybrook Farm over here at my desk. Just to say that there is now no negative voice in my head shouty enough to stop me from writing completely. That wasn't the case for the first, I'm going to say, ten or fifteen years of my writing career. Maybe longer. I can't say when it went away, but I can say that it did go away. From which we can conclude that it *does go away.* So keep your eye on that. Be aware which voices within you have the power to grind your writing to a halt.

Maybe write those voices down. Definitely trust that they'll die down.

Okay, back to pivots. *A father is waiting for his daughter to come home from a date.* What's the pivot? The moment she gets home, right? Or maybe when she calls. The detail doesn't matter. Right now all that matters is the information in its purest state. Let's say he's apprehensive, he doesn't know if she's safe. Now he gets a phone call, "Dad, I'm alright," and now he's relieved. See that? He goes from apprehensive to relieved, a nice little arc of change across the pivot of new information: How does dad feel prepivot (or maybe just pre)? *Apprehensive*. Post? *Relieved*. And the pivot? The new information: "Dad, I'm all right."

(Do you know what drives me crazy? *Alright* and *all right*. After all these years I still don't know which to use. And don't tell me to go to the internet for the answer. Yes, we can all agree about the nature of consensus reality, but the real problem lies inside me. I feel like I've used *alright* forever, and never felt all right about it. Alright? All right. It was just on my mind.)

Okay, so now we understand that pivots are a certain kind of glue: they bond action to emotion. To get a feel for how this works just jot down a few. 1) Assign an arbitrary state of mind, 2) introduce new information, 3) change the state of mind. Easy as 1) 2) 3), thus: A man is happily getting a haircut; the haircut sucks; now he's unhappy.

Okay, so if pivots are the building blocks of story, what happens when you string a bunch of them together? Duh, you get a story. Start by creating a character and giving her a state of mind. Then give her a pivot and change her state of mind. Then do that again. Then do that again. Then do that again till you're done.

Please, Dog, don't get me started on dyslexia.

I'm laughing. I don't know where that line came from. Oh, wait, yes I do. I was about to say, "Please God, don't get me started on *till* versus *til*," but then I wrote Dog by accident and hilarity ensued. I'm pretty proud of that little joke. But guess what? *Now I'm off the page!* Now I'm not thinking about the work, I'm just sitting here *shining* – a word I take to mean in this context feeling super good about myself. As we're already aware, negative feelings impede writing. It turns out that positive feelings can, too. Right now I'm daydreaming about how great it's all going to be when it's done – how much you'll love this book and email me to tell me (jvx@vorza.com). Now, there's nothing wrong with feeling good, except that it's distracting. When I find myself shining too long or too much, what I do is *I take the win*. I bask in the moment momentarily, then tell myself to get over myself and get back to work, on the simple logic that you'll never email me to tell me *anything* if I never finish the book.

If you're wondering, I do also spend unproductive time thinking about how much you'll *hate* this book and email to tell me *that*. I recognize that I'm exposing my ego to a lot of potential punishment (*we agree, JV, get over yourself*) and believe me that grieves me. But I can't shut up. I'm here telling you that the best way to be the best writer you can is just to present yourself – your unvarnished true self – to the world. How can I teach you that if I'm not willing to model it? Or let's put it this way: if it has to do with my writing process and I'm thinking about it, you're hearing about it. Take from that what you will.

Where were we? Oh yeah, pivots. If you're wondering where to find them – these magical new pieces of information that create new emotional states – the good news is they're all around. You're bombarded by pivots all day every day. You just don't think of them that way.

I go to the post office, I'm hoping for a short line. But the line is out the door. Now I'm cranky.

Now you.

The Boston Red Sox mount a late rally! Pivot! Elation! But they still lose! Pivot! Despair!

Now you.

I'm going to stop saying now you now. Assume that it's always your turn.

To get good at using pivots, get good at mapping emotions. Become practiced at asking, "What is this character feeling now?" Then think of something that would change that feeling into something else — anything else. Change of emotional state, by the way, is what gives meaning to action. Without it, you just have a cartoon. Or no, not even that, something flatter than that. Because even in a cartoon, when Wile E. Coyote goes over a cliff, that's certainly a pivot. Pre, he was happily in hot pursuit. Post, he's in mortal terror. So even cartoons have pivots. Even tweets. Can you tell a pivot-driven story in just 140 characters? I'm betting 140 characters you can. Remember, it's always your turn.

So what happens when pivots are missing? Nothing. I mean literally nothing happens. You just have people sitting around drinking coffee. Making observations. Maybe making jokes. But not moving a story forward and not investing action with meaning. What falls out from this is that pivots are handy not just for generating creative content but also for testing what you've written. If you can see the pivots, you have a story; if you can't, you don't.

A guy is waiting for the bus. He's still waiting for the bus. And still waiting.

This is a moment in need of a pivot. The bus comes and the guy gets on. Is that the pivot? Not until he realizes that the driver is a *zombie!* Now you've got a story. Or the driver is *his ex-wife!* Now you have another story. Or the driver is a *supergenius criminal!* Now you have another story. You think you're going to run out of story? Never. Not ever. Not so long as action and emotion exist.

This example tells us something important about the relationship between action and emotion. In some sense, the new information should be *unexpected.* If it's expected, it doesn't drive sufficient change of emotional state. I've heard it said (I know I've heard it said because I've said it), that writing stories is just this easy:

Just never have things happen as planned.

What happens when things go as planned? Nothing. The story stalls because emotions remain unchanged. So that's bad. But never fear, it's really hard to stall a story for long, and it will get harder as you go. Wow, that was stated pretty clumsily (as was that). I just mean that once you see pivots as the substrate of story, and once you understand your story as merely a long string of emotional states changed by new information, you'll find that you get less and less lost, and your stories have more and more drive. You can look forward to that.

I took a break just now, and had something to eat. Since my eating habits are ridiculous, I ate standing up at the sink, watching TV. I know: *me, huh?* Anyway, there in everlasting reruns was the Fresh Prince of Bel-Air. And darned if he wasn't confidently expecting victory on this TV quiz show when an unexpectedly tough rival showed up at the last minute, and there went his confidence. Good ol' Will Smith, pivoting just for me. So, as His Freshness reminded me just now, a TV story is nothing but pivots. You can build your whole structure on that.

But that's going to take some trying, huh? So let's get trying, huh? Start stringing pivots together. Just make things not happen as planned. You can take any common situation... the commonest... a guy walks into a bar...

A guy walks into a bar. What's his state of mind? Let's say *hopeful to hook up.* Somebody toss me a pivot. Yes, right, of course: he sees a girl. What's his emotional state? Oh, enthusiastic. And yes, of course we will have to investigate her emotional state, too. At the end of the day you have to track all your characters' emotional states, but first get good at following one character through story, and get good at following one at a time. If you try to follow too many at once, well, that's another good way to get lost. Keep it simple for now.

So, his emotional state is enthusiastic. Next pivot? *My God,* (I almost wrote *my Dog,* tee hee) *she comes up to him!* Oops, now he's scared. And optimistic. But she just wants to meet his cute friend. New information; pivot to disappointment. But wait, there's another girl, so... joy again! And on the story goes and grows.

Couple of points. First, there's nothing wrong with repeating an emotion if it's appropriate to do so. Just there in that bar, the guy passed through joy twice, and I guess that's the point of the story: to showcase his indomitable spirit. Anyway, Heraclitus said you can't enter the same river twice, and that dude was right on. The joy a character feels early in a sequence of pivots must necessarily be different from the exact same joy he feels later. Also, while big emotional reversals are both useful and easier to see, you don't have to place a premium on big emotional change and you don't have to swing your characters' state of mind from pole to pole. Sometimes an emotional state… just… deepens, as would be the case in taking a character from scared to scared shitless.

But the main thing is, don't try to control things too closely. Let your characters tell you their emotional state. Let it be authentic to them. A womanizer – oh, hell, let's make it a manizer – will apprehend a bar much differently from someone coming off a broken heart, and different again from, let's say, someone who's never been in a bar before. But here's what you may not know: You already know every emotion all of your characters ever will. Because you've experienced them all yourself. You have a full and complete inventory of emotions – it comes as standard equipment. Now just withdraw them from inventory and assign them to characters as you see fit.

Action and emotion. What happens and how people feel. That's really all story is. That's all you need to know.

Do yourself an exercise. Write a stack of sentences that are all action and emotion, and not anything else. I'll go first, but rather briefly, for this is your exercise, not mine.

Jack walks into a dark room. He's scared. The light comes on and everyone yells surprise. He's surprised. His wife gives him a kiss. He feels love. His friends offer good wishes. He feels loved. He drinks champagne. He feels buzzed. He meets a sexy single woman. He feels flirty. They hit it off. He feels sexy. They start kissing. He feels aroused. His wife catches him. He feels caught.

Couple of things. First, again, I'm writing without judgment, or at least with as little judgment as I can manage. I mean, I don't really like Jack. Already he seems like a creep and what's worse, I feel like a creep for inventing him. But I can't worry about that. *You can't worry about that!* There will come a time later for wondering whether the sentences you've written are the right ones. The trick now is to drive a story from action to emotion, emotion to action, action to emotion, and start getting good at that.

Also note that this room is just a room, free of even a single descriptive, bar dark. This so relieves clutter on the page. At the right time in the development process you would dress up Jack's room, describe the furniture, the people you see, fill it up with detail. That time, though, is not now. Now it's just action, emotion, action, emotion, action, emotion, until you get the hang of it. You can go do that now. Give it a whole page. I'm happy to wait.

I've used that joke before, you know, that *I'll wait while you do the exercise* gag. I used it in *The Comic Toolbox,* in poker books and elsewhere. That's something else I'm trying to get over, my taboo against recycling. I have to get over that. Some jokes bear repeating. Some ideas bear resharing. Not just recurring themes, although themes do profoundly recur, but also trivial stuff. I've used the phrase *mayonnaise motherfucker* in almost every novel I've written. I seem to find places it fits. Ah-ha! And I seem to have no taboo against recycling after all. Well, while you were doing your exercise, I just learned something new about me.

So how did a page of pivots feel? What did you learn about you? About the way you see action and interpret emotion? I imagine that at some point you felt inefficient or blocked, maybe self-censored in some sense. I suppose that at some point you felt good about your choices, about how freely your text flowed because you didn't care about outcome. I hope that at some point you got high, because if you don't know it, the writer's high is a *huge* part of why we're all here. We'll come back to that.

Did you see yourself write? What did you learn about your voice?

I'm thinking about my voice. I'm thinking that my voice was my voice all along and I just didn't know it. I mean, I always knew I had a point of view, and I knew I had a form of expression, but nobody ever told me it was my specific job as a writer to develop those things, focus on and showcase them. What someone did tell me (hi, Richie Raskind) was don't be afraid to write stuff that some people hate; if people don't get worked up one way or another, you're never going to have any kind of career. Well, that might not be true. You could write *aaalll* about puppies, and who doesn't love puppies, right? But think about *Hamlet*. Greatest work of English lit, but some people hate it. I hate it, because every time I look at Hamlet's choices I just want to shout, "Stupid Hamlet, don't do that!" I find that yelling at Hamlet does no good, but the point is, I am engaged. That's a story I care about. I'm not saying *write to piss people off,* but up till now you may have been saying *don't write to piss people off.* You set something free when you try.

So then pivot down a page again, only this time go for something rougher, something that a development executive would call "edgy" without having the slightest idea what she means. Go for an aggressive voice. Try to antagonize, just to see how that feels. Break your rules and taboos. Take yourself places you *know* you don't go. For just a page. Half a page. Did I mention I'm not keeping score?

No one's keeping score. That's the other part they don't tell you when they turn you loose (or you turn yourself loose) on the writer's path with no sense of what to expect. Left to your own devices, you're *bound* to keep score. But that's just silly. Your writing's not good, your writing's not bad, it's just the writing you're doing now.

It's not that none of what you write is crap. For a time in most writers' lives, much is. But that passes. Meantime, get used to being wrong on the page. Get okay with it. So you can get on with your work.

In other words, feel good about writing bad. It's easy to do if you remember that your writing always serves the twin goals of advancing the current work and advancing your craft. Even when the writing doesn't advance the work it still builds craft. Never get down on yourself for a day of bad writing. Every day, every hour, every minute you spend writing, even the worst, builds craft. Builds it in a way you can bank on, and expect to collect dividends on later on. Take it from me, you'll get better. You'll get so good you can't even stand it.

You're getting better already, hadn't you noticed? By using strategies and not caring about outcomes you're growing your craft. By using action and emotion you're growing stories. You have permission to fail and some reasons to feel good about that. The rest is just putting in time.

I'm getting excited for you. I can't help it. I really believe this stuff is that easy. This sentence here is a *piece of cake!* This one too. (This one not so much.) You want it in math? Here's math: ***If you want to get better, write more. If you want to get a lot better, write a lot more***. Write more and don't care. Use such strategies as present themselves, but mostly just don't care. Because *that* will allow you to write. And *some* of what you write will be damn good. And then more. And then more. And the parts of the process that vex you now (maybe just the act of sitting down at the desk) will vex you less and less. This happens gradually and it happens naturally as you build your active practice.

It was in, I'm going to say, 1986, that I tried to write my first novel. That was a *huge* ask. How did I *dare* to write something large as a novel? I tricked myself into it, that's how, by signing up for a three-day novel writing contest. Maybe you've done something like this. If you haven't you should try, here's why: If you set out to write a novel in three days, you won't expect it to be any good and you won't have any time to care. After three days, you'll have something that looks very much like a three-day novel – and you'll have had three *very* enlightening days in your craft.

My three-day novel was called *Antlions.* It opened like this:

> This is Jan Tesch. She's almost eighteen years old. She has dark blonde hair that she wears in braids.
>
> She weighs 102 pounds soaking wet.
>
> She's soaking wet right now.
>
> It has occurred to her that the Cascade range of mountains probably got that name for a reason. She has a hunch it's got something to do with rain. Right now she's trying to have as little to do with rain as possible, which means huddling against a slightly slanted slab of granite, wishing to hell it had the decency to be a cave. She entertains fantasies of finding the magic switch which will open the secret door. She finds that fantasies of this sort are useful to a girl out standing in the rain. Let a smile be your umbrella? Jan says let a fantasy be your pup tent.

Oh, the merry I could make in telling you about the computer I wrote that novel on, an IBM PCjr, the dinosaur of the computer age, with no hard drive and programs that ran from 5.25" floppies. I was constantly playing chicken with file corruption. If I didn't save my work in sufficiently small files, I risked seeing the text turn into something like this.

> Meninø raî tï hió garbagå bag®   Hå pulleä ouô á wateò ☐

I'm not making this up. I absolutely am not. With just 256 k – *k!* – of memory, the computer would frequently crash and such hideousness would ensue. It was horrible. Horrible to see the work of a day reduced to gibberish. But *such* an improvement over longhand or typewriter, because now, suddenly, with the tap of a delete key, I could make mistakes go away. If I really think about it, I'd have to say that as much as anything else in my writing life, the delete key set me free.

Anyway, a three-day novel under fraught circumstances, but I got to THE END, and that was a blessed event. Did I win? Of course I didn't win. Who wins a novel writing contest with sentences like Meninø raî tï hió garbagå bag®   Hå pulleä ouô á wateò ☐?

And by the way, this is another artifact I've held onto for long, long years. With every new computer I've ever owned, I have simply carried all my work forward, so that finding a quarter-century old file took me mere seconds, here at my desk. I figured out early on that a hard drive doesn't care how many versions you save. My advice is *save everything.* In digital form it costs nothing and weighs nothing, and it'll be there when you need it, or when you never need it.

So, me and my *Antlions.* I'll bet if I went back through it I'd find dozens of jokes or thoughts or turns of phrase that I've used dozens of times since. And this is something else nobody told me and I really wish they had: None of it's wasted. None of it. I've had bunches of broken stories that lay fallow until I got good enough to fix them. And even absent such acts of resurrection, hey, an active practice of writing means writing *a lot.* As we've already noted, repetition is par for the course. As you advance as a writer, you build up a body of work. Then you start mining that body of work for the things you need, and I'll tell you right now: the stuff that's a direct lift, that's a small part of it. Mostly what you mine is your experience of writing what you wrote before. The mistakes you made and the lessons you learned. The tricks you taught yourself, and then taught yourself to repeat. That's the stuff you mine, and that's why none of it's wasted.

I'm trying to think of a trick I taught myself, and then taught myself to repeat.

Oh, here's a good one.

When I start my writing day, I find it useful to reread what I wrote the day before. Trouble is, if I'm not careful, that can easily turn into a whole day of rewriting what I wrote the day before. At a time when I'm trying to get to THE END as quickly as possible, that's counter-productive and I don't want to do it. So the only key I allow myself to touch is the one that says *page down*. That lets me reread what I wrote, and reacquaint myself with the story I'm telling, without getting bogged down in editing that I don't want to do right now. It's a good way to ramp myself up for the day's work. Try it and see if it serves you, too.

3. WHAT TO DO ABOUT WRITER'S BLOCK

Almost the minute I started writing, I started wasting time, on everything from emails and Minesweeper to Xbox and stupid frucking Freecell. I'm not alone in this. All writers waste time. Sometimes we do it because we're not quite ready or able to solve the story or script problem at hand, and we need more time to let our thoughts marinate. Often, though, we squander our hours because we are afraid. Some writers spend their entire lives at this, rather than ever commit to putting words on the page. I didn't want to be one of those guys, so early in my career I came up with this handy motto:

Procrastinate later.

And that was helpful, it really was. It reminded me to start my writing day with the writing and save the screwing around for afterward. No two words advanced my practice of writing more swiftly and surely than "procrastinate later." They might do the same for you, so the next time you have a choice between doing the work now and doing the work later, try opting for now. That's good practice, but it only solves half the problem, because that's what happens when you *can* write, and it's just a question of when you choose to do so. But what about when you can't write at all? What happens when the whole paradigm breaks down and you find yourself sort of just staring at the screen, lost? That's kind of a sucky feeling, isn't it? It has a name we know and loathe, writer's block, and every writer I've ever met has suffered from it at one time or another. If you're not among that number then you are unimaginably blessed. For the rest of us, writer's block is a thicket of stalled progress, and it would be useful if we could find our way out.

Fortunately, we can. The exit is marked in just two words:

Don't Write.

Wait, what? Don't write? How can not-writing possibly solve the problem of not being able to write? Isn't not-writing exactly the issue? What the hell has Vorhaus been smoking?

Vorhaus has been smoking nothing. Vorhaus knows that writer's block takes place at the specific intersection of *too much fear* and *not enough information*. Imagine two busy streets with poor traffic control and many Russian drivers. Collisions happen frequently here. They're often messy and never pretty. Let's break it down.

When confronted with a difficult creative problem, one that makes us struggle, the feeling may naturally creep in that, oops, this is a problem we can't actually solve. Maybe it's a joke that eludes us, a knotty plot twist, an emotion we only imperfectly understand, or a situation or scene we can't quite visualize. Whatever the cause of this consternation, it drives us (like a speeding Russian Lada) to the brink of our creative insecurity and leaves us staring into the void. At this point it often happens that apprehension becomes an albatross, a weight of dread draped around our necks. This apprehension keeps us from writing – literally stops us cold – because how we can do effective creative problem solving when we're bent under the weight of so much self-doubt? The creative self looks at itself and says, "Yikes! I truly suck!" This creates an insidious negative feedback loop. We fail creatively. Then we see ourselves failing creatively, which undermines our confidence. Absent confidence, we fail some more. Witnessing more failure, we clutch up even worse. Next think we know, we've seized up and broken down. Like a Lada.

And that's what writer's block really is: not the absence of words, the presence of fear. You've pulled a metaphorical muscle – your creative muscle – and now that muscle is in crisis, spasming and cramping like all get-out. Not a party with candles and cake for you.

Interestingly, the thing that triggers this vicious circle is usually just not knowing enough about the creative problem we're trying to solve. We haven't sufficiently stoked our inner engines with the right kind of data. Maybe we need more research about the world of our story. Maybe we need to deepen our understanding of our characters. Maybe we need to broaden our search for interesting pivots. Maybe we just need to go deeper into ourselves, more thoroughly mine our "inner data," and figure out what the heck we're trying to say. Whatever information we're lacking, it's the lack of information that stops us cold. If you don't believe that's true just ask yourself what you'd be doing if you *did* have enough information to solve the problem.

That's right, you'd be solving the problem, without fear and without doubt. You would be in creative command.

When you're *not* in command, that's when you stand at the intersection of too much fear and not enough information, there among the speeding Ladas. And that's when you get to take the radical advice, ***if you can't write, stop trying***. Just stop. Put down your pen. Walk away from the keyboard. Go do something else instead – and that specific something else is this: *gather data*.

In the world of my dim understanding of human physiology, I've been led to understand brain function, broadly, as *left is for logic, right is for rock 'n' roll.* Well, right now, the rock 'n' roll side of our brain, the creative side, just isn't working. But the left side, the logic side, is working just fine. We may doubt that we can write (we may doubt that we'll ever write again) but we don't doubt that we can look shit up. So that's what we'll do here. We'll look shit up. We won't fear failure because information gathering engages the left side of our brain and it doesn't engage the ego. Therefore, when writing is hard but harvesting data is easy, don't do the hard thing, do the easy thing instead.

Now watch the magic happen. Over here, your left brain is gathering information. Because this is easy, your brain starts to relax. That terrible creative cramping starts to subside. Fear diminishes. The right brain's overwhelming paralytic feeling of *I suck forever!* now fades away, ignored by a left brain that's focused on something it does easily and well. The creative muscle comes out of spasm. What's more, all that new information acts on it like catnip. Before you know it, you're making new connections, new discoveries, processing new information in ways that get you re-engaged with your work and excited by new possibilities. Next thing you know, you're writing again. Simply, efficiently, effectively, automatically. And all because you made the decision not to write when writing was hard to do.

Let's make it step-by-step, shall we?

1. Recognize that you are blocked. (How will you know? Duh, you're not writing.)

2. Stop trying to force your way past the block. (That will just yield yucky results and make you feel worse.)

3. Go gather some information. (Seek both external and internal data sources. Sometimes the answers are already in your head and you just need to look at them more closely.)

4. Relax your brain. (Your ego stops tormenting you because, hey, any ol' ego can gather data.)

5. Find yourself back writing again. (Yay.)

6. Repeat as necessary. (And it will be necessary; new problems always lie ahead.)

So there you go. Writer's block sorted, forever and ever, amen. Don't thank me, I define myself through service.

Now let's talk about a different type of information: the feedback we get on our work. Here again we're going to see that there's a dynamic relationship between information and ego, and if we can get a handle on that relationship, we're going to do an altogether better job of using feedback effectively.

Start by asking yourself this question: When you give your work to someone and await their notes, critique or opinion, what's the best you can hope for and what's the worst you can fear? If you're like most of us (and by most of us I mean me) the best you can hope for is, *My God, that's genius! Don't you dare change a word! Ever!* And the worst you can fear is, *Uhm, dude, maybe you'd just better never write.* I'm here to tell you that neither of these emotions is particularly useful, because they focus on our feelings and not on the information. We can do much better than that.

Were I able to draw, I would just now be drawing something like a big barrel, which I would label *information,* and I'd have a tube or pipe coming out of it that then split in two, so as to lead either to a filter labeled **serve the ego** or one marked **serve the work**. There would be a valve you could turn to control which way the information flowed, through the filter of ego or the filter of work, as you saw fit. I might paint the valve chartreuse, just because I can.

When you filter through *serve the ego*, you're asking the question, "How does this information make me feel?" When you filter through *serve the work*, you're asking, "How can I use this information to improve my results?" As you can imagine, filtering through ego takes your attention off the work and that at minimum will slow you down, even if the information makes you feel good. But don't forget that the ego has a natural desire to defend itself by ignoring or rejecting information that makes it feel bad. That will hurt your efficiency even more since, in terms of sheer utility, you can't process any information until you acknowledge it and accept it, which, thanks to filtering through ego, you might not be doing at all.

No problem, right? Just flip the valve the other way and filter through **serve the work**.

Easier said than done, you say? Wrong, I insist; exactly *as* easily said as done. Just make a choice. And not even the choice *never* to ask, "How does this information make me feel?" but only to save contemplation of that question for later. Maybe you feel attacked, forlorn, sucky, whatever – *think about it later.* For now just focus on how you can use the information you're receiving to help close the gap between where the work is and where you want it to be. There's absolutely nothing wrong with feeling what you feel when someone gives you news about your work. It's just not particularly productive. In the case of bad news – the kind of news that causes defensive shields to go up – it's downright counterproductive. But even good news (the kind of praise that makes your ego feel all warm and fluffy) can have a negative impact on your work, simply because it distracts.

Take me, for example. We already know that I like to shine. If you give me good news in the form of praise for my work, I will shine like a [metaphor left to the reader]. But if I shine too hard I may miss important information behind your praise. So I make a choice to serve now and shine later. I get the information I need and the work improves. Now here comes the good part. When the work improves, how do I feel about myself? Better? You betcha. So if my goal is to feel better about myself as a writer, I'll get there much faster if I simply make the conscious choice to focus on serving the work, and trust that by serving the work I will improve the work, and get to feeling that much better that much faster.

In other words, **to serve the ego, ignore the ego**.

In other other words, **save your ego for the award ceremony.**

Remember, it's just a matter of choice. This may be a choice you don't have much experience with (most people filter through ego by default) but it's one you can *gain* experience with, and get better at, just by recognizing that the two different choices are available to you, and then by being sufficiently self-aware to make the one you want to make in terms of how you filter information.

The information we're speaking of here includes the input you receive, and will receive, from readers, editors, agents, publishers, producers, and the ever-loving public for as long as you live and write. What I'm proposing is that you set yourself the goal of remaining *emotionally neutral* to that input. Don't think of feedback as criticism; also don't think of it as praise. Just think of it as information – information you can use to do better the things you're trying to do well.

True story: A million years ago when I was first writing sitcom spec scripts, my wife was my editor. We weren't married then. (We were together for seventeen years before we got married. Somebody asked was the sex better once we wed, and I say, "Well, *yeah*, 'cause we *waited*." Can I get a ba-doom-tish?) She gave me notes on a script and of one joke she said, "I don't get this."

To which I replied, true story, "Then you must be stupid."

I know: *me, huh?*

Anyway, see what happens when you filter through ego? If you do something dumb like lash out, you not only waste the available information *(duh, the joke didn't work)* you risk losing your editor – and maybe your lover. All it cost me was a night on the couch, but I deserved it. I was a dick.

Do I assume that your editor and your lover are one in the same? That's not a given, of course, but also not a terribly bad assumption. After all, your editors have to come from somewhere. You don't want to use overpaid experts like me if you can help it, or worse, overpaid experts *not* like me, for they will be both overpaid and unhelpful. So then, where will your editors – your beloved and vital beta testers – come from? Where will you turn for information about where your writing is and isn't working? Lovers and friends, friends. Fellow writers in classes or groups, sure, but what you really want is someone who is *devoted* to editing you, someone who has a vested interest in helping you improve. When you find such a person, trust me, you do not want to alienate her.

Now, I've been dining out on that "you must be stupid" story for almost three decades. Teaching from it. Illustrating what bad things can happen when you drive information through the filter of ego. It always gets a laugh, but it also always makes a point. If you say *ouch, my feelings* every time someone gives you bad news about your work, A) you'll drive those people away and, 2) your work will cease to evolve. So filter input through service to the work. It's not easy but it's not impossible. It's the sort of thing you can make a habit, and grow as a habit over time.

After my ego-driven worst, I strove to become more emotionally neutral to input. I'm still not perfect, but I'm a whole lot better than I was. And you know what? As with your practice of writing, if you practice being good at taking feedback, you simply can't help but improve. As recently as yesterday I got a note from the editor of my next novel pointing out that I ended four consecutive chapters with variations on the same line, and that this was boring and repetitive and would have to change. Folks, I try to be my own best editor, but this was something I completely missed. Where would I be without an editor I can trust? Exposing my mistakes to my readers – the *last* people I want to see them. And where would I be if I were harsh and rejective of my editor? Without an editor. And that would be bad.

So take it as read: Over time, you get better. You start to understand how important feedback is, and how useful. Or just get more used to taking it. You become more workmanlike – and one can't help but wonder, if "workmanlike" is a workmanlike word, what is a word like "workwomanlike" like?

Can you see how much fun this book is for me? Can you dig the shit I'm letting myself get away with here? Maybe you're thinking, *Man, JV, you need an editor,* but me, I'm thinking, *This is a fun ride.* And how did it get fun? By me getting out of my ego's way. I stopped laboring over *how much all this matters* and everything got easier from there. You can, too. It's like turning on a light. After that it's just practice.

So here's how you practice. Take that page of pivots you wrote (or anything else you wrote) and hand it to someone close by. Ask what they like and what they don't. Ask them to be as specific as possible. No matter what they say, no matter how it makes you feel, be emotionally neutral to the feedback you receive and process it as pure information. Did you connect with your words? Did you get a laugh (or a tear)? You need to know where and how that happened so you can do it lots more. And your editor just told you. Does your story lose steam? You need to know where and how that happened so you can do it lots less. And your editor told you that, too. Now you're getting served. You're being given (for free!) vital information about what you do well and what you do less well. You can consider this fuel for your writing engine. In fact, it's supercharged fuel, because I guarantee that anyone who cares enough about you to serve you in this way will make for good company, and who can't use more good company?

Serve the work. Don't serve the ego. So many good things happen from that.

4.　THE PRACTICE OF PRACTICE

If you're a writer, you write. Nothing else matters. You can be the worst writer in the world, spewing drivel onto the page every day, but if you do it *every day,* eventually it will cease being drivel, or at least evolve into drivel of a finer sort.

This happens automatically, because if you write you always improve, which, obviously, if you don't you won't. So that would seem to leave us with a pretty clear choice, wouldn't it? Write, and improve; or don't write, and don't improve. Why is it not that simple? Because of the need to write good. Burdened by the unrealistic expectation of *all quality all the time,* we often find that we *just can't write at all.*

But in the practice of writing, quality is not the major concern. The major concern, as we've already learned, is words on the page. Nothing else matters but that. So how does one practice *practice*? How can we constantly be closing the gap between the writer's life we have and the writer's life we want? Here are some strategies and tactics you can try:

PRACTICE PATIENCE. Some days you get a ton done. Some days you don't. You'll tolerate the bad days better if you just *let yourself off the hook.* Stress and pressure are not conducive to good writing practice, so go easy on yourself. Life is long. You do have time.

PRACTICE IMPATIENCE. If yesterday was a slack day, make damn sure that today isn't. Yes, it's okay to blow off work, but not every day, not if you're serious about your craft. Let yourself off the hook, sure, but put yourself back on it, too. Demand your own active participation in your active practice of writing.

SET APPROPRIATE GOALS. Don't imagine that you're going to write a whole novel or script before breakfast. Do imagine that you're going to do a reasonable amount of work in a reasonable amount of time. Inappropriately large goals kill will and crush productivity. Appropriately sized goals offer the immediate reward of a job, well, done.

SHOW YOUR WORK. Be fearless in this. Recognize that rejection is a natural part of the practice of writing. You don't have to like it, but you do have to accept it. And while we're wrapping our brains around the oxymoronic *accept rejection,* let's remember that the alternative is a trunk full of stuff that no one sees till you're dead. And then no one sees it ever, because who, really, will want to wade through the stuff in your trunk?

SEIZE YOUR SPACE AND TIME AND TOOLS. It's difficult to have an effective practice of writing in an ineffective space. Do you have a quiet place to work, equipped with decent writing tools? If not, make it a priority to acquire these things. Also make your writing *time* a priority. Carve it out of your day, guard it jealously and don't let anyone – especially you – take it away from you. In the early days of my practice I found it useful to set library hours. Sentenced myself to them, it felt like sometimes. But it put me in a time and space where the writing took place and I needed that.

LET YOUR LIFE RISE. The practice of writing can be (I think should be) one of constant revelation. In becoming the writer you wish to be, you naturally undergo major transformations in terms of the person you are. Let these changes take place. As you gather awareness, you improve as a writer; as you improve as a writer, you gather awareness. Let your life rise and your writing will follow; let your writing rise, and your life will follow, too. And that's pretty groovy if it's true, and it is.

Writing isn't easy, but it really isn't hard. You put a word on the page, then another and another (and another and another) and soon you have some words on the page. You struggle to encode your thoughts in language, and soon you find that you've encoded effectively; your words are understood. You try to grasp deeper meaning with elegance and power, and by degrees you learn how to do it. With time, with patience, with *effort,* the practice of writing emerges from the desire to write. Over time, after much effort, the practice of writing becomes second nature, as much a part of your life as breathing. It's not just a goal you can achieve, it's one you certainly *will* achieve, if you only keep writing.

So now let's practice *keep writing.* Maybe say for the next week you'll track your time at your desk and see if you can bump up your practice by, what, 23 percent? If you do that, I'll let you in on the secret of the number 23. It's one every writer should know.

No, I'm not going to tell you now. Instead I'm going to talk about the gift.

5. HAVE A THEME

You became a writer because you had something to say. Own and cherish that something. It's your gift, and your gift to others. That's why around here (in the land of many sayings) we have a saying: ***Keep your heart where everyone can see it***. The more actively and openly you promote your vision, the clearer your vision will become. The clearer your vision becomes, the better you can communicate it. And if you don't know it now, you soon will: Your passion for communicating your vision will overcome all fears.

And all that stands between your passion overwhelming your fears is, uh, your fears overwhelming your passion. Weirdly, by some strange emotional math, you fear to be free of fear. How does that work? If you're like many writers, it works like this: Every time you think about truly speaking your mind on the page, a dark little voice in your head says, "Hold on there, pardner. Who do you think you are, telling other people what to think?"

I'll tell you who you are: You're a writer; it's your job to tell people what to think.

If you don't believe it's your job, let me ask you, have you ever gotten a creative high? Of course you have. We all have. It's one of the big reasons we write; we get off on it. What we get, specifically and chemically, is the endorphin explosion that comes in the midst of a great writing jag. And *endorphin,* if you don't know, is short for *endogenous morphine*. So let there be no illusions: Our brains are juicing themselves with onboard opiates. Why would they do such a thing? Because they're trying to get us hooked on acts of creation. Our brains, if you can imagine such a thing, are treating themselves like rats in an exquisite lab experiment – *press bar, get treat*. Every time we create, we turn ourselves on. Why should that be? Why do our brains reward us so heavily for engaging in the creative act?

Because it's good for us. For you. For me. For that guy over there. For anyone and everyone. For all us naked apes stumbling around on this planet, just trying to survive. Creativity helps us do that. Creativity is profoundly pro-survival. Creativity has directly and indispensably helped humanity adapt and evolve ever since the first person looked at two sticks and said, "Fire? Why the hell not?"

So creativity is pro-survival and creativity is rewarded by the brain. Where else do we see this dynamic relationship? In risk: It's good for humanity that you take chances, and you get paid in adrenaline when you do. Also, sex. Has to feel good – great! – or we wouldn't do it. Which would be bad for the species in general. Eating, same way. You eat, you feel good. If you didn't feel good, you wouldn't eat. If you didn't eat, you'd die. So all of these pro-survival activities are generously bribed by the brain. And there's creativity right up there with them. What does that mean for us as writers? This: We're not the ones rubbing those sticks together, but we are the ones spreading the word. And when everyone knows how to make fire, that's thanks to us. So when we state the truth of our experience, when we write what we think is important or necessary or true, when we say what the world is, how it operates, how it *should* operate, we're really just doing a writer's job: spreading the word; the word as we understand it.

Which is just what everyone wants writers to do anyway. Look, there's two kinds of people in this world. Us writers, and everyone else. We inform, and they are informed. They look to us to *be* informed. They reward us when we inform them – reward us with money or praise or appreciation or fame – and that's everyone from the winner of her local poetry slam to Stephen Frucking Spielberg who's such a great storyteller that he gets to be Stephen Frucking Spielberg!

The brain rewards us for having a thought. The audience rewards us for sharing that thought. That's a pretty powerful set of forces siding with us. What do you have to do to side with them back? Not much. Just tell the truth when you write. The truth as you understand it. Nothing fancy. Nothing forced.

Just the truth you believe in and want to promote. Place that truth – or those truths – at the heart of your stories and you'll never run short of something to say and you'll never stop getting high when you do.

So what exactly do you want to say? The answer to that question is your *theme.*

I find it easier to think about that question by putting it this way: If you had the magic ability to open up someone's brain, anyone's or even everyone's, and slip an idea in there and really make it stick, what would that idea be?

For me it would be *be whimsical.* Today at least, I can think of nothing more important than that. So today, what can you think of nothing more important than? (Another champion sentence there, JV.) What do you want people to do or be or think? Forget the taboo against ordering people around, or at least ignore it for now. Just let your imagination flow. If you could change people, *really* make them believe or behave differently, what would you tell them to do?

Hey everybody, *stop killing each other.*

Or, hey everybody, *find someone to love.*

Or, hey everybody, *follow your dream.*

These are instructions. These are the things we call themes.

A theme is a truth we believe in and want to promote, expressed as a call to action.

Hey you reader, when you're done reading this book, here is what I want you to believe: that you can be a writer of fabulosity beyond your wildest dreams. My theme for you, my instruction, is *go be that writer*. And my story will be one of someone who becomes that writer, which you are helping me with by taking your own writer's journey. So we're in this together, writer and reader, and that's the reader/writer partnership all the time and every time.

A partnership driven by theme. Writers write to explain stuff. Readers read to figure stuff out.

Now I'm going to ask you again. What truth do *you* want to tell? Have a good long think. Write some words down. Commit your beliefs to a page of explanation and see what that feels like. I'll bet if you stick with it for even a page you'll get at least a little bit high, because with these words you are tapping into the really important stuff about being a writer – not how a plot works but about your deepest, truest sense of yourself – and that's when your brain rewards you the most. As for how the audience will reward you, let's leave that for now. For 99 percent of the writing process, the best thing to do with the audience is ignore it, because contemplation of the audience takes you off the page. It took me off the page just now. But I'm back, so let's move on.

That exercise you just did? Thinking of your most super-important theme and writing a heartfelt page about it? Do that again ten times with ten different themes. There's no law that says you can't have more than one most super-important theme. In your career you'll need lots. So get good at seeing them everywhere. In the relationships of people around you. *Hey mom and dad, stop fighting.* In your social philosophy. *Question authority!* In your sense of self. *Take a stand!* In your heartfelt desire for others. *Take a chance!* All of these things are your themes. You can call it your set of values if you like, but this isn't so much about promoting your values as it is about centering your stories.

Remember that themes are imperatives – calls to action. "Truth" is not a theme. "Tell the truth" is, because it tells us what it wants us to do. Likewise, "love" isn't a theme until you tell me what you want me to do with it. Find it? Fight for it? Not live without it? Your instruction on the subject is your theme. And your theme centers your story. It tells you how to tell it.

Let's see how that works.

You start with a theme. Let's say something fun, like *have fun.*

Next you build you a hero, where *hero* is not a person of epic proportions but just who the story's about. It could be you. Your neighbor. A soldier. A dog. The second undersecretary for development in Western No Guinea, an island you just invented.

Now here's the simplest definition of story I know. ***A story is an arc of change from denial to acceptance of the theme.*** At the start, the hero is in denial of the theme. At the end, she's in acceptance. She has undergone change, a specific change directly in relationship to the theme.

So if the theme is *have fun* and the hero is the second undersecretary for development in Western No Guinea, where do we expect to find her when the story starts? Correct: not having fun. We don't know why. At this point we don't care. Where do we expect to find her at the end of the story? Right again: now she's having fun. We don't know how she got there, and again we don't care. We don't need those details now. Now we just want to see the story in its barest of bones:

Theme.

Hero.

Arc of change.

Denial.

Acceptance.

The second assistant undersecretary for development in Western No Guinea goes from not having fun to having fun. That's a story, a story driven by a theme.

It's easy as Mad Libs if you think about it. The theme of the story is [insert theme]. The hero is [insert name]. The story is [*name* learns to *theme*].

The theme is *make friends*. The hero is *Lonely Jack*. The story is *Lonely Jack learns to make friends*.

Wow, that looks like an exercise you can do ten times quick.

Me and my *ten times* exercises. Why am I such a slave to decimals? It's always been that way, you know. In *The Comic Toolbox* I invented the Rule of Nine, which says that for every ten ideas you try nine won't work, which is excellent news when it comes to not over-investing your ego. If you know that 90 percent of everything you come up won't make the cut, you get very comfortable with seeing stuff fail, which helps you relax. Plus, you get an outstanding rationale for generating more stuff: at this rate you'll need lots. But why Rule of Nine? Why not 12 or 23? This I do not know.

Must be something to do with the number of fingers I have.

Write a bunch of themes. Get good at that. Get unafraid to speak your mind. Recognize that you're just doing your job.

6. INDY PUB

When I was a kid writer, we had vanity press and it was beneath contempt. In my first or second apartment I had a landlord who self-published this hideous hardback mystery with the title and a gold gilt eyeball embossed on its blue cardboard cover. I don't remember the title but it was uuuhhhnnnreadable. You can just imagine the style: flat, derivative, cliché, self-indulgent, dumb, sadly lacking an editor and desperately showing the need. Since this type of so-called literary so-called output was so common in vanity press, where the only way to get something published was to pay for it yourself, it was easy to believe that people who self-published must be, by definition, unself-aware creeps.

That's a pretty harsh assessment, and maybe that was just me, my own fear of being an unself-aware creep, but whatever. Even so, and even after all these years, to me, and maybe to you, vanity press is risible. And yet I self-publish. Dude, I self-published this. So what does that say about me? That I got over it. I got over it by realizing that editors at publishing houses are not the only arbiters of quality. Yes, they're gatekeepers of a sort, and yes they do keep the most egregious of texts from gratuitously abusing dead trees. But mostly editors and publishing houses have historically served as a means to an end: the (formerly) most economical and efficient way of putting books in people's hands.

Of course, all of that has changed. It changed for me in a personal, visceral way the day I went into a Barnes & Noble bookstore looking for a copy of my then-new novel, *The California Roll.* Not finding it in stock, I thought I'd order it because I understood (according to the mythos of the past) that by bringing my book to the attention of big distributors, I would ensure its place in the distribution chain. Well, do you know what the sales associate did? He went to a computer and commenced to order my book from the B&N website, *just as I would do at home.* That's when I realized that the old model of bookselling was dead as eight-track tape. That's when I realized I needed a new model. A new model with a new name.

Not *self-publishing,* with all its excoriative scorn. Rather, *independent publishing,* or *indy-pub,* which makes me feel like a radical new rock band no one has heard of. For psychological reasons, I draw heavily on that model. Rock bands figured it out long before writers. Just because they were on their own label didn't mean they sucked. It meant they'd found a way around a clumsy, cumbersome distribution system that no longer met their needs.

I've said it before and I'll say it again: More often than not, rules are made by rule-makers for the benefit of rule-makers. If those rules don't benefit us, we don't have to follow 'em. The old distribution systems, for music and for books, made things *very* good for publishers and distributors, but not so good for artists and authors. New tools have overthrown old rules. Now anyone can find an audience. All they have to do is try.

The world we live in now is one of digital natives and digital immigrants. Digital immigrants are people like me, folks whose living memory goes back to rotary telephones and black-and-white TV. Digital natives are people (like most of you readers, I suspect) who grew up in the age of iEverything. Ideas that I find strange, or struggle to accept, come as naturally to you as falling asleep.

So maybe you don't have this big mental barrier against self-publishing. Maybe you don't have to call it indy pub to make the taboo go away. If that's true, more power to you. Now the question is, what will you do with that power?

What's different about today, dear digital natives, is that when it comes to independent publishing, you no longer have to pay to play. You can indy pub without spending a dime, and you can get paid. No, I'm not suddenly going to turn this book into a teaching tool for the mechanics of that. I'm sure you can find your way to Kindle Direct Publishing and

Createspace all on your own. I'm more interested in the question of what you will write, how you will fill that space – how you will storm the citadel of publishing now that the gatekeepers can no longer hold you back. It's a precious beauty, isn't it? The freedom to write, and distribute, any damn thing you please.

Only, please, not so fast.

Not so fast with your master's thesis or your collection of poetry (or God help me, my precious *Antlions.*) Not so fast with your poorly conceived and utterly un-proofread collection of short short stories. Not so fast with your collection of tweets. We're not going to vanity press this. We're going to be thoughtful. We're going to frame the problem and solve it, give ourselves a target we can actually hit. Let's start by setting some parameters.

The thing you will write (if you do this daunting exercise) will be somewhere in the neighborhood of 10,000 to 20,000 words. That's not nothing, but it's not a novel, for which the minimum length (of a self-respecting one, at lest) is around 70,000 words. Yet nor is it an essay left over from your college anthro class. So the thing we're talking about is not a day's work, it's many days' work. More to the point, it's the minimum word window at which you can start leveraging the power of distributor-free publishing and actually sell works online. It's also – and this is emerging news – rather the favored length for a lot of readers these days, enough readers to constitute a market. This may be a function of everybody's shrinking attention span, or a function of the fact that your ebook reader also contains Angry Birds.

So now you know how many words you'll be writing – enough to charge $4.99. And you know who you're going after – people who snack on $4.99 reads. This is obviously not the only market a writer can attack, but the thoughtful writer attacks all her markets this same way: by thinking them through.

Are you thinking this isn't your market, this indy-pub short book I'm proposing you write? Are you, let's say, a screenwriter by self-definition and not really interested in writing prose? Okay, then maybe this exercise isn't for you. But pretend it is, because part of advancing your craft is trying out forms and genres you don't consider naturally your own. So embrace the exercise. Set out just to explore another way of writing. That can't be bad, right? Don't worry about whether you indy pub it or not.

In fact, let's all not worry about that. It'll take us off the page.

A good thing about this word range of 10 to 20K is that it's easy to write – much easier than a novel or a screenplay, or a history, biography, memoir, whatever fills the space in your writer's mind labeled, *This is the big one! Maybe too big for me!* Ten thousand words *isn't* the big one. And it knows it's not. It's an achievable goal, a target we can hit. That's why we set it.

So, now, what kind of creative works add up to a minimum of 10,000 words? Short stories or collections of stories. Essays or collections of essays. Novellas. Tightly focused nonfiction. Memoir. Humor. Nonsense –

Okay, let's pause on nonsense. Suppose you set the goal of writing 10,000 words of nonsense. How long do you think it would take you? Geez, you could do it as fast as you can type – it's just nonsense. You could probably crank out the pure verbiage in a day, but that's not the point, because of course you don't want to write nonsense. You plan to invest more care. If I were you I would plan it like this: a thousand words a day for ten days or as many days as it takes. And while I wouldn't set out to write nonsense exactly, I would let nonsense live, because this is a first draft, and that is the nature of those. Because immediately after these ten days come another ten days of rewriting a thousand words at a time. After that you've got something that's been attended to. That's the work of a writer who's practicing her craft.

So now you know the writing proposition you face: call it a month's worth of work. That seems reasonable, a goal you can set and achieve, and one that will help you grow your craft. Now you have a word range and a deadline, and you have some genre options.

How will you ever choose among them?

By using something called a *decision-making matrix*.

Draw a table, a simple grid of maybe ten by ten (there's my slavish devotion to decimality again). Down the left side of the table list parts of the writing process, or types of writing, that you're good at. Across the top, list things you might enjoy writing, or writing about. Then check all boxes that apply. Look for the ideas that leverage most of your strengths. By this simple means you'll figure out which projects you're likely to be good at and also likely to enjoy.

Like, I'd love to write a brief history of the Iran-Iraq War, 1980-1988. I'm fascinated by the subject, and it would be perfect at that length for a kickass overview. But I know I'm never going to do it, because I hate research like a cat hates baths, and I know I'm no good at it. So I look for other ideas.

When you think about your writing strengths, think about your knowledge strengths, too. What do you know about that most people don't? You have one huge asset already: your themes. Nobody knows them like you, so knowledge of your themes is something you can definitely claim as a strength. You might also be good at humor, dialogue, "what's happening now," and tech stuff. Some of that is "writing strengths" and some of it is "other." Hell, I don't know, maybe you know how to bake brie.

(Which means that you can write a great indy-pub book on baking brie, while I cannot.) When I started writing works of this length, I knew a lot about poker and a lot about obsessive collecting, and I leaned heavily on those strengths to get me over the specific hurdle of feeling comfortable writing prose. Example:

> *Just in the sports books alone you've got Super Bowl shot glasses, Derby Day souvenir wallets, World Series watches, cheap and digital, but cool and collectible with the baseball face. Or the poker room with high-hand hats and bad-beat crying towels. When it's free, it's apt to get left behind. In my long experience of collecting, something of everything always gets left behind. Like slot cards that earn comp points on slot play, redeemable for discounted show tickets or free meals or yet more key chains and coffee mugs. All the time you see people join the slot clubs, play the pull toys, then forget their pretty plastic cards in the electronic card readers. Then I swing by and collect them. I've been at it for years. I collect coin tubs, what you put your quarters in when you win. Some I store, others I use to hold promotional pins and chips that I've found. Or slot tokens. If you look, you'll see: tokens get left in trays.*

> *I could play them back into the pull toys, but I'd rather collect them. It's what I do.*
>
> *There's this joke they tell on people like me, about a magazine called* Obsessive Collector's Monthly *and its special souvenir edition...*

Write what you know say the pros, and it makes sense. If you haven't written longform before, you're bound to feel nervous about it. You will feel less nervous if you write within some area of authority or expertise.

So *stuff you know* is a strength. What else is a strength? Make a list. Check it twice. Don't imagine you're short on strengths. You'll see plenty if you just give yourself five minutes to look. Then list what you might like to write. A story about chickens? If that's what comes to mind. Me, I'd be listing: that Iran/Iraq thing I just mentioned; a chunk of my memoir, *But It's Funny In Russian*; something philosophical; a quick and dirty book called *Lies, Idiots and Dumbass Wars;* and of course...this book here. I told you it was a metalogue. You are reading the result of my own decision-making matrix.

Suppose your strengths are: religious belief; an eye for detail; compassion; special knowledge of teenagers. And the things you'd like to write include: a guide to Chinese cameras; a political treatise;

transformative youth fiction. You'd choose youth fiction, right? And yes I stack the deck with these choices, but I do it to illustrate how easy this is. List what you're good at. List what you'd enjoy writing. Look where they intersect. *Write that.*

The decision-making matrix, by the way, is a tool you can use for lots more than just writing. It's handy for choosing everything from to wear (comfortable + looks good) to what sort of job to go after or where to meet new people. Or you could use it to match your strengths to market needs. Product developers use it all the time. I use it to decide what to have for dinner. Try it and see.

Then sit down and write. Seriously, folks, it's no good just *reading* about writing. You have to do the homework. It's where the benefit lies.

7. THE LAW OF KEVIN

Can't find a story to tell? Try knocking out a thousand words on this one, ripped from yesterday's headlines:

> A nun was charged with stealing roughly $128,000, which she then gambled away on casino visits. Sister Mary Pseudonym faced felony grand larceny charges after allegedly misappropriating funds from two small churches. Diocese officials referred the matter to local law enforcement after discovering the theft of parishioners' contributions. Sister Pseudonym, aged "about 50," had previously received unspecified treatment for a gambling addiction, according to local reports.

Ready, set, go! It practically writes itself!

Or actually, as you just discovered, it did not write itself. You did that. You made a decision to sit down and bat out a thousand words on anything at all, just to experience yourself doing it. When you did that, you engaged your practice of writing. You grew your craft. May I cheer your effort once again? Once again: yay you.

So we know that building our active practice of writing is simply a matter of spending time in the game. We recognize that time is scalable. You can write a limerick in an instant on a beer mat (ooh, try that – it's fun). To tackle a thousand words about nothing, that's an afternoon's work. To map out the 10 or 20k words we talked about above, that takes a bit more planning and, at my estimation, a month. When you engage something really longform, like a novel or a screenplay, that's a commitment. That's going to become part of your life. Something you'll have a relationship with. So write what you love, obviously, and give them you, obviously, because if this next thing you write is going to take up a year of your life, you damn sure want to make sure it makes your life rise. Give it thought and careful consideration. Weigh your alternatives. Use a decision-making matrix to help. Pick a project that harmonizes with where you are now as a writer and where you want to go next. Be thoughtful and analytical in this. To engage a longform work is to make a commitment. Make it to something that's worth a commitment, something worthy of the sweat and work and worry you plan to put into it. Something worthy of your love.

At the same time, don't worry *too* much about your choice. (Certainly don't worry about it so much that you never write anything – that would be counterproductive.) No matter what you write, no matter how poorly or well, you're bound to learn something profound, something that will help you grow as a writer. You want to be on the lookout for that in works of all scale, but especially the longforms, for they cost so much in terms of time and effort, and sometimes pay small (or no) dividends in terms or audience or sales. You have to have something else to take away from those writing experiences, otherwise you might go mad. If you get nothing else, get the education. Remember always that every word you write serves two goals: advancing you toward the end of this task; improving your ability to do this job.

Pick a project.

Pick a start date.

Pick a time frame.

Set a deadline.

Now you're a writer.

Except you're not really a writer until you're a rewriter. So let's look at how we can get good at that, too.

First, recognize that it's hard for writers to let go. It's hard for everyone. It's even harder for sitcom characters. If you take a close look at the best ones, you'll see that they're guided by something the Germans call *feste Vorstellung,* a firm or fixed idea. This idea, this cherished belief, defines the sitcom character's worldview, and it turns out that he'll do pretty much anything he can to get outer reality – everybody else in the known universe, that is, plus the known universe itself – to concur with his cherished belief. Sheldon on *The Big Bang Theory,* for example, believes that he's everyone's intellectually superior and will do anything – abuse or neglect other people, damage his own career, even bring himself personal bodily harm – in order to prove that thesis. Comic characters, by and large, do not work to advance their own self-interest. They work to advance their *feste Vorstellung.*

We are not comic characters (by and large) and we've learned to strike a balance between self-interest and self-image. In the name of self-interest, a writer should seek the fastest and most effective path to a successful story, script, limerick, haiku, whatever. Yet if you put two writers together in a room, chances are you'll soon see them fighting over ideas – fighting mainly over whose idea gets to be best. Then watch cooperation fly out the window, driven away by the unconscious need to protect the hidden cherished belief that *I'm the best writer in the room.*

This is, of course, another instance of serving the ego instead of serving the work, but it goes a little bit deeper than that. As it happens, we writers often over-commit to our ideas not because we think they're the best ideas, or even particularly good ideas, but just because they're *our ideas*. I have codified this phenomenon as something I call *the Law of Kevin,* a concept I am absolutely, stunningly, eternally in love with, well, just because it's mine.

I invented the Law of Kevin some years back while running a writing workshop in Geneva, Switzerland. I was trying to make the point – this very point right here – that it's just terribly easy for writers to become emotionally attached to their words on the page, even when those particular words aren't particularly important. To illustrate the point, I had two students come to the front of the room and write an arbitrarily selected character name – Kevin – on the white board. Then I asked them which version of Kevin they liked best, and each admitted that she liked hers best. Note that this wasn't a joke or a story beat or anything. It solved no particular problem and required no particular creativity. It was just a character name, arbitrarily arrived at and handed to the writer. Yet it still placed on both of them the pull of pride of ownership. And that's this creative block in a nutshell. If we can't let go of even a character name, how will we ever let go of a story idea or a theme or a scene or even a joke?

It helps to remember that so much of what we write *is* Kevin: text of not particularly great importance, except as it serves as a platform for something else. And the problem of overcommitment to Precious Kevin is not just an issue for writers. I have seen administrative assistants fight over whether the cells of a spreadsheet should be yellow or orange, not because they thought their color was prettier or cooler, but just because, again, it was *their choice.* We get married to our choices. In all walks of life, in any line of work. We do. And until we learn to loosen up on that, we have a hard time moving toward goals, creative or otherwise.

So here's what you have to do.

You have to kill Kevin.

Kill Kevin. Kill him again and again. Rather than fight for a joke, or a story idea, or the color of a cell in a spreadsheet, just let it go. What you replace it with will be better, I promise. Why? Because the next idea will have the platform of the last idea to stand upon. Your next choice is *always* more informed than your last choice, precisely *because* of your last choice. The new choice always has the old idea to stand upon and draw from, and that's a huge help. This, though, is not always easy to see, thanks to a little something called *the hill climbing problem*.

The hill climbing problem is a way of viewing a situation or challenge or choice, and a means of negotiating with yourself, or others, to make a short-term sacrifice for the sake of a long-term gain. It's useful for writers facing catastrophic rewrites. It's also surprisingly useful, as we shall see, for writers who are contemplating quitting their jobs or other significant life changes.

Here's how it works.

You're standing on the top of a hill, a nice little metaphorical hill with a beautiful, sweeping metaphorical view. Smooth, round top, this hill; lovely white pines, maybe some clover. A cavorting bunny or two. Not a bad hill as hills go – but it's only a hill. Meanwhile, off there in the distance you can see a mountain, a majestic metaphorical one. And, cavorting bunnies notwithstanding, you know, just *know,* that on top of that mountain is where you really want to be. In writing terms, the mountaintop is the place where great writing resides. In whole-life terms, the mountain might represent freedom, the place you get to go when you make the decision to let all your life choices, or at least certain key ones, be yours and yours alone.

Now, from your hilltop vantage point you can't see a clear path leading from the hill to the mountain. Yes, there's a path leading down off the hilltop, but it descends into a valley filled with, let's say, fog that obscures the path. It'd be great if you could just fly straight to the mountaintop, or even teleport, but the laws of physics and gravity rule this metaphor, so you become aware that if you ultimately want to go up, you must start by going down. This is a challenge – the heart of the hill climbing problem, because most of us don't easily let go of our gains. Your gain, in this case, might be a story or script that half works, but won't fully work without a page-one rewrite. It might be a job that pays pretty well but ignites no passion. Whatever it is, it's kind of okay, it kind of works, and the hill climbing problem demands that you let go of it for the promise of something better. Trouble is, that promise is uncertain. You can see the path down from this place but not necessarily the one up to a higher place. For many people, here's where inertia sets in. They can't trade existing gains for that uncertain promise of more. So they stay put. They camp out on the hilltop and try to persuade themselves that cavorting bunnies are really all they need.

As hilltops go, it's not a bad one. It should be enough.

But it's not enough. It never is. Not for true creative strivers or for anyone authentically yearning to see their lives rise. If that's you – if you want more and demand more from your life than the "just okay" hilltop you're presently on – I propose the following logic:

If you don't leave, you'll never arrive.

Faced with that choice – certain stagnation or uncertain success – true strivers find their way down off the hill, even unto the fog below.

People make creative investments, and they can be pretty stubborn about holding onto them. Part of this is Law of Kevin stuff, but part is really just the honorable sense that, *Hey, I've put in my hours. This should have borne fruit.* Maybe for you it's a script that opens really funny and sexy but then completely falls apart. This is very common among script writers at a certain stage of their development. They can write great beginnings and kickass middles, but haven't yet mastered the art of the elegant ending. Well, here's the problem with that. Those great beginnings and kickass middles often set up endings that simply will not work. Maybe the story is broken, or maybe it sets up an expectation that just can't be met. Then you're in a situation where "that dog don't hunt," and the only solution is to tear everything down and rebuild it from scratch. Informed by the notion that *if you don't leave you'll never arrive,* you come down off the hill and head for the mountain, not necessarily with faith that you'll reach it but just because you'd find it intolerable to stay stuck on the hill.

Real writers find it intolerable to stay stuck.

In fact, people with real passion for anything find it intolerable to stay stuck. Maybe you have a kickass job, and maybe it even pays great. If it's not…I don't know...sculpting giant pandas out of Philadelphia cream cheese or doing play-by-play for a minor league baseball team or whatever really floats your boat, sooner or later you will find that you have to leave it behind. Could you do it? Could you really give up a decent job just because it didn't sufficiently scratch your urgent itch to create? Many people do; I did. I was assistant creative director at an ad agency, at a fairly tender age, and scared myself straight out of that job with the logic that I didn't want to find myself still there at 40, still "making the world safe for advertising." In quitting that job, I relinquished not only cash and security, but a certain self-image as someone who needed security (and cash). The choice redefined me, but at the time it seemed no choice at all. I was damned if I'd stay on that hill.

I don't want to say that you're trapped in your life. I'd hate to say that you're trapped in your life. But if you *feel* that you're trapped in your life (or even just trapped in a first draft of something that you know could be lots better if you just let lots of stuff go), recognize the hill climbing problem as your way out of that trap. Sure it's a difficult road, and sure you might not succeed, but if you don't go somewhere then you'll just get nowhere, and for real writers – writers like you, I am quite sure – that's a prospect too horrible to entertain.

8. SPACE AND TIME

There's a certain homework assignment I give in every writing class I teach. "Between now and next class," I tell my students, "go out and do something you've never done." I don't give much more information or definition to the exercise than that, because part of the fun and the utility of the assignment is figuring out just what the hell it is. Left to their own devices, students routinely do the homework in predictable ways.

Some don't do it at all, and claim that by not doing the homework they're actually doing it because, hey, they've never *not* done a homework assignment before. They think they're being clever, but really they're just being scared. And that's a shame, because they're missing out on a great opportunity – the rare and wonderful opportunity to break some rules. It doesn't come around often enough for people in this orderly society of ours, writers and non-writers alike, but the experience has much to offer.

Some who do the exercise treat it quite lightly. They kiss a stranger or buy a stranger a drink. That's fine as far as it goes. It's not exactly life-changing, but they still get the buzz of seeing themselves in a different light. They get to experience their own boldness, and they find that it gets them off.

Sometimes, people embrace the exercise on its deepest level. One woman used my homework as an excuse to have a civil conversation with her ex-husband – something she assured me she had never, ever done before. I like to think that my little homework changed their whole way of being with one another. At minimum, and at least temporarily, it changed the sorting system in her brain. It let her feel free.

The highest grade I ever gave on this assignment was to a young guy in Rome who rode the bus to class reading a hard core porno magazine as if it were a newspaper. When I asked him how he felt, he said, "At first, scared. But then I realized that everyone was giving me plenty of space. They were scared of me. So then I felt powerful. By the time I got off the bus, I just felt high."

So there's our theme again: There are some things you should do in this life just because they get you high. Taking risks, breaking rules, engaging in acts of creation, these are the means by which we grow, not just as writers but as human beings. So here's your homework. Between now and when next we meet, go out and do something – anything – you've never done before. Find out how it feels. Don't be afraid to be outrageous. You have my permission.

Finally, let's talk about two things every writer needs: space and time.

Writing space is not the issue it once was. With a pair of headphones and a power supply, your space can be anywhere. Mine, too, but it didn't used to be that way, you betcha. My first "office" was a kitchen alcove, no, not even that, a corner, a nooklet. With three TV trays for a desk and some badass Koss Pro 4AA headphones with coffee-can earcups and a padded headpiece that could withstand hammer blows. Man, you were locked in in those things. And when I put them on, everyone knew – mostly I knew – that this was writing time and Johnny was not to be disturbed.

Because that's the issue, isn't it? You're not to be disturbed. How you negotiate that with others is one thing, but the first how do you negotiate it with yourself? To be a real writer takes time. How do you carve out the time?

There are practical considerations. You need a job to get by, I get that. And yes jobs take time, but not *all* your time. Though the excuse of them might. When you come off a long shift, a long anything, it's easy enough to say that you're tired, that the writing can wait. Or to use the excuse of last night's late night to keep you from writing right now. Or laundry. A broken limb. Sometimes these excuses are completely legit, but *sometimes* you're just padding a rationale around your fear to write. Fear not! Be serious-minded in pursuit of your craft. Set your schedule, stick to it, and earn your self-respect. Put in your time. Don't let you take it away from you.

And don't let anyone else, either. This can be tricky. People can have legitimate demands on your time, and that's everyone from your lover or spouse to your kids, your friends, your *dog,* that list goes on. But sometimes – you have to remember this – sometimes those demands *aren't* legit. Sometimes you give them legitimacy – *I can't write now! I have to change my mom's light bulbs!* – and you need to learn not to do that. Worst of all, it sometimes happens – this is another hard truth – that those around you don't *want* you to write. They don't want you to succeed in building an active practice of writing. I hope that's not your situation, because it's about the hardest one for a real writer to deal with. But let's take a look at it, so you'll know it when you see it.

Suppose you were exactly who you are, exactly where you are, a writer building her active practice. You're closing the gap between the writer you are and the writer you want to be. How does that look to the people around you? They may be just jealous of the lost attention, if that's attention that you would otherwise have given it to them. But it might go deeper than that. They might start to feel threatened because you're closing in on your dream and they're not. It's hard for them (some of them) to feel good about that. They might find it easier, or at least less threatening, to thwart your growth than to face the lack of their own.

A lifetime ago, a guy told me that, "You're either on the road or you're in the swamp." I assumed he meant *road to enlightenment* and blah, blah, blah, and he did. "For people stuck in the swamp," he said, "they don't like to see others escape. It makes them feel bad." I wish I remembered who that guy was. He had another interesting idea about the road and the swamp. He said that people on the road were never attracted to people in the swamp because that's a place they've left behind. People in the swamp *want* people on the road, but can't attract them because, you know, swamp. So if you want to attract enlightened, hard-working people into your life, you kind of have to be one of those.

Enlightened company: just another perk of the writer's life.

In any case, fight for your time. Don't forget that sometimes you'll be fighting yourself. In the meantime, for those around you who are well-meaning but just unused to the idea of you being the kind of writer you want to be, a little frank talk is called for. Just tell them what you plan for yourself, invite their support, but stake your claim and stick to it. If they respect your goals, they'll grant you the time and space you need. If they don't respect your goals, that's a larger problem, and one I can't address right now, though maybe next time.

In rethinking this subject just now, I realized that I was falling victim to a hidden assumption, the assumption that writing time is, or should be, a consistent value from one day to the next. I practice an orderly routine in which the writing starts at a certain hour and ends at a certain hour, every day if I can manage it. But you might be different. You might be the writer's retreat type, bingeing on your craft when you get the chance. Hey, maybe you're even sneaking your sessions, either at work or… *"Honey, I'm going to Starbucks!"* (But really you're going to Starbucks to *write!)* Or something completely else, I don't know. And anyway that's not my job. It's up to you to look at you and figure out how best to structure your practice of writing. I'm sure you can do that by now.

There's so much more I want to talk about. How writers and editors can build a common vocabulary and a common code to lubricate their co-creative work. How to attract (and be) an excellent writing partner. The importance and utility of teaching what you know. Ten tips (*ten – sheesh!*) for writing dynamic dialogue. The secret significance of the number 23. I suppose I'll tackle them all in *How to Write Good Volume 2: How to Write Gooder.* But this book is over, executed according to its design, for better or worse. I hope you have a lot of highlighted passages. I hope you have a lot of sticky notes. If I were going to remember three things from this text, they would be these:

Have a theme.

Serve the work.

Keep giving them you until you is what they want.

Beyond that, be humble in your expectations. Be generous with your words (in other words, write lots). Be generous with your spirit. Hold onto everything loosely. Always make room for the new idea. Be patient with yourself but rigorous with your practice, for that's how you grow, day by day, hour by hour, word by word. Have a clear understanding of your goals, and please have them not be *get rich and famous.* As I can tell you from here, from the intersection of *not starving* and *somewhat followed on Facebook,* there are paths to sublime writing success that have nothing to do with being rich and famous. For the sake of your happiness, take that idea on board.

I always say that my goal is to be a better writer today than I was yesterday, which I now know from long experience happens purely as a function of putting in my time. I can look forward to being a better writer on the day I die than on any day prior.

I wonder what I can look forward to the day after that.

ABOUT THE AUTHOR

John Vorhaus is the author of seven novels, four books on writing, ten books on poker, and one book on strip poker. He also travels extensively, teaching and training writers worldwide (29 countries on five continents at last count). His motto and business model is, "Walk down the beach, pick up everything you find, and turn it into a party hat." He tweets for no apparent reason @TrueFactBarFact and secretly controls the world from www.johnvorhaus.com.

Printed in Great Britain
by Amazon